MAYER SMITH

Behind the Gold and the Grit

Copyright © 2025 by Mayer Smith

All rights reserved. No part of this publication may be reproduced, stored or transmitted in any form or by any means, electronic, mechanical, photocopying, recording, scanning, or otherwise without written permission from the publisher. It is illegal to copy this book, post it to a website, or distribute it by any other means without permission.

This novel is entirely a work of fiction. The names, characters and incidents portrayed in it are the work of the author's imagination. Any resemblance to actual persons, living or dead, events or localities is entirely coincidental.

Mayer Smith asserts the moral right to be identified as the author of this work.

Mayer Smith has no responsibility for the persistence or accuracy of URLs for external or third-party Internet Websites referred to in this publication and does not guarantee that any content on such Websites is, or will remain, accurate or appropriate.

Designations used by companies to distinguish their products are often claimed as trademarks. All brand names and product names used in this book and on its cover are trade names, service marks, trademarks and registered trademarks of their respective owners. The publishers and the book are not associated with any product or vendor mentioned in this book. None of the companies referenced within the book have endorsed the book.

First edition

This book was professionally typeset on Reedsy. Find out more at reedsy.com

Contents

1. The Decision — 1
2. The First Step — 7
3. A New Face — 14
4. Struggling to Fit In — 21
5. Emma's Secret — 28
6. A Moment of Weakness — 35
7. Dangerous Consequences — 42
8. The Unraveling — 49
9. The Wade — 56
10. A Reckoning — 63
11. The Truth Comes Out — 70
12. The Fallout — 77
13. A Chance at Redemption — 84
14. A Final Test — 91
15. New Beginnings — 98

One

The Decision

The city's skyline was a breathtaking canvas of glittering lights, stretching endlessly beyond the horizon. From his penthouse suite on the 43rd floor of one of the tallest buildings in the city, Alexander Moore gazed out over it all—his empire, his kingdom. The view was the epitome of success, a picture-perfect scene of opulence and power. Yet, as his sharp blue eyes reflected the brilliance of the lights below, they seemed far removed, distant, like a man who had no connection to the world he ruled.

Alexander had it all—wealth, power, a life of luxury and privilege. He was the CEO of Moore Enterprises, one of the most influential corporations in the country. His name was synonymous with success. Every meeting he attended, every deal he made, had been a step toward greater dominance in his industry. But at this moment, none of it mattered. The success that had once exhilarated him now felt hollow.

He stood at the large glass window, watching the cars move below, the bustling streets filled with people—faces that he would never know, lives he would never touch. A gnawing emptiness tugged at him, a relentless ache that he couldn't shake. He had everything most people dreamed of, but he felt as if he were standing at the edge of a vast abyss, staring into nothingness.

The phone on his desk buzzed. It was the personal assistant he never needed, a voice on the other end, pleasant and efficient. "Mr. Moore, your dinner appointment with Mr. Parker has been rescheduled to 8:30 p.m. Would you like me to confirm the details?"

He didn't respond immediately. His gaze remained fixed on the city lights below, the steady rhythm of the world continuing as if it had no place for him. His mind was elsewhere, thinking of something—someone—he hadn't thought of in a long time.

"Cancel it," he finally said, his voice almost distant. "I'm not going."

"Of course, sir. Shall I reschedule the next meeting with Mr. Parker?"

"No. No more meetings." Alexander hung up the phone and collapsed into the leather chair behind his desk. He let out a slow breath, his fingers trembling slightly as he loosened the collar of his expensive suit.

The Decision

His gaze drifted to the framed photograph on the desk—his father, standing beside him at the ribbon-cutting ceremony for Moore Enterprises' headquarters. His father's sharp eyes glimmered with pride in the photo, but Alexander knew that pride had been built on expectations, not love. He could still remember the long hours spent in the office, the constant pressure to be better, to be more. The sense of duty that had been instilled in him, the need to live up to the legacy his father had built.

But it all felt so insignificant now.

He turned his chair slightly, glancing at the stack of papers that had been waiting for his signature for the past few days. They were the same papers he'd signed without a second thought in the past—contracts, financial statements, acquisitions—but now, they seemed utterly meaningless. The life he had built was suffocating him, and he knew it. He had everything, yet felt nothing.

A thought flickered through his mind—a fleeting whisper, almost like a dream. What if he could escape it all? What if he could disappear, slip away from the life he knew and live as someone else, someone who wasn't burdened by the weight of expectations?

The thought lingered, settling into his mind like a seed waiting to be watered. He leaned forward in his chair, his hands clasping together tightly. He didn't know where the thought had come from, but it felt right. More than that, it felt necessary.

"Maybe it's time for a change," he whispered to himself, his voice barely audible in the silence of the room.

The decision was sudden, but in that moment, it felt inevitable. Alexander Moore—billionaire, CEO, master of his world—was going to give it all up.

He pushed back his chair and stood up, moving across the room. His reflection in the glass was a stranger to him now. The tailored suit, the perfect haircut, the confident posture—it all felt like a costume, a façade he had been wearing for far too long. He ran a hand through his hair, staring at the reflection as if trying to recognize the man who looked back at him.

"Who am I really?" he muttered under his breath.

He thought of the people he'd met in passing—those who lived in neighborhoods far from his gilded cage. People who didn't measure success by the size of their bank accounts or the opulence of their homes. People who fought every day just to survive. They had something real, something Alexander felt he had lost—purpose, connection, authenticity.

In that instant, a plan began to form in his mind, one that seemed reckless, even insane. He was going to walk away from his fortune, his legacy, everything he had built, and live among the people he had always looked down upon. He would leave behind the world of boardrooms and luxury cars, of designer suits and expensive champagne, and step into a life that was raw, unpolished, and real.

The Decision

He would hide his wealth, assume a new identity, and immerse himself in the life of someone who had nothing but the clothes on their back. It was a ridiculous idea, he knew. But it felt right. He had to know what it was like to be ordinary, to feel what others felt—to live a life free from the burden of his wealth and title.

It was a dangerous decision. The risk of being discovered was high, and the consequences could be catastrophic. But in that moment, he didn't care. He was tired of playing the role. He was tired of being Alexander Moore, the billionaire who could never be himself.

The thought of doing something completely out of character, of shedding his identity like a snake shedding its skin, thrilled him. It felt like the beginning of something new, something that could give him the answers he was looking for.

He walked to his desk and picked up the phone. His assistant would arrange everything—his resignation from Moore Enterprises, the transfer of his wealth into an anonymous account, and the new identity he would assume. He would disappear from the public eye, vanish into the world of the common man, and see life from their perspective.

"Mr. Moore?" the assistant's voice crackled through the phone.

"Prepare the paperwork for my resignation," he said, his voice steady, though his heart raced. "I'm leaving."

There was a pause, a moment of confusion, before the assistant responded. "Understood, sir."

Alexander hung up and took a deep breath. The weight of the decision began to settle on his shoulders, but for the first time in years, he felt something other than dread—he felt exhilarated.

Tomorrow, he would leave it all behind. Tomorrow, he would become someone new.

And he would never look back.

Two

The First Step

The morning sunlight streamed through the large windows of Alexander Moore's penthouse suite, casting long, golden shadows across the polished floors. The city outside had already begun to stir—cars honking, people bustling on the streets below—but inside, it was a world untouched by time.

Alexander stood by the window, dressed in a simple black shirt and dark jeans, no sign of the suit or polished persona that had once defined him. His face was unshaven, his hair unruly, a far cry from the man he had been only a few days ago. It was only a matter of hours now before he would leave this life behind. The decision had been made, and there was no turning back.

He glanced at the briefcase on the table, filled with cash and documents under a false name. It felt foreign to him now, almost absurd. This wasn't the world he was accustomed to, and yet, he couldn't help but feel a rush of excitement every time he looked at it. His heart was pounding, adrenaline coursing through his veins. This was it—the first step toward becoming someone else, someone free from the constraints of wealth and legacy.

His phone buzzed, breaking the stillness of the room. It was his assistant, Maria. He had prepared her for his departure, but still, the weight of the conversation loomed.

"Good morning, sir. I've prepared the documents for your resignation as discussed," she said, her voice cool and professional. "Would you like me to handle the public announcement?"

Alexander paused, staring out at the city. A brief moment of doubt flickered through him, but he pushed it aside. There was no room for doubt now. He had made up his mind.

"No, Maria. I've already taken care of everything. It's time to disappear," he said, his voice steady but with an underlying tension that even he couldn't deny.

There was silence on the other end for a moment, and Alexander could almost hear the hesitation in Maria's response. "Understood, sir. I'll have everything finalized on my end. Good luck with… everything."

With that, the call ended. Alexander pocketed the phone and took one last look around the penthouse—the life he was about to abandon. It wasn't just the physical space he was leaving

The First Step

behind; it was everything that came with it—the fame, the influence, the power. All of it was about to be erased, and he couldn't help but wonder if he was making a mistake.

But then, the thought of living a life untethered, unbound by his fortune, reignited the fire within him. He was doing this for himself—for the freedom to experience life as it was meant to be lived, with no strings attached, no expectations.

He grabbed his bag, checked the contents one last time, and left the penthouse. The elevator ride down was eerily quiet, and for the first time in years, Alexander felt like a stranger in his own skin.

Outside the building, he stood for a moment, watching the world go by. The streets were as busy as always—people rushing to work, children running toward school buses, vendors selling their wares on the corner. But now, he was just one of the crowd, anonymous. He was no longer the man with a name that everyone knew; he was simply another face in the sea of strangers.

His driver had already left, and there was no need for the luxury car he was used to. Instead, Alexander hailed a cab, and for the first time in his life, he experienced the humbling feeling of waiting for a ride like an ordinary person. The driver pulled up, an older man with graying hair and a tired smile.

"Where to?" the driver asked, his eyes meeting Alexander's in the rearview mirror.

"Just drive. I'll tell you when to stop," Alexander replied, his voice low.

The cab merged into traffic, and as the car moved through the streets, Alexander couldn't help but feel a sense of surreal detachment. This was the beginning of his new life, but it felt like he was floating in some strange, dreamlike state. The city he had once dominated now seemed distant, as if he were watching it through a foggy window.

After what felt like an eternity, the cab pulled up to a small apartment building in an area far removed from the high-rise towers and luxury neighborhoods where he had lived. The area was quiet, almost too quiet, with graffiti on the walls and the unmistakable scent of neglect in the air. It was the kind of place where people lived because they had no choice—not because they could afford better.

The driver turned to him. "This is it, then?"

Alexander nodded, handing the driver a wad of cash before stepping out of the cab. He stood on the curb, taking in his surroundings. The noise of the city seemed far away now, replaced by the distant hum of life in this underprivileged neighborhood.

For a moment, he hesitated. This was real. There was no turning back now. His mansion, his sleek office, his trusted associates—none of them could help him here. He was alone. And yet, there was something freeing about it. He didn't have to be Alexander Moore anymore. Here, he could be anyone.

The First Step

He walked into the building, the door creaking slightly as he pushed it open. The hallway was dimly lit, the air stale and thick with the scent of old carpet and mildew. His footsteps echoed in the narrow corridor as he made his way up the stairs, the sound growing louder the higher he climbed.

At the top of the stairs, he found his new apartment—a small, one-bedroom unit that was worlds apart from the luxury of his previous life. The door was unlocked, and as he stepped inside, the silence hit him. The apartment was sparsely furnished, with only the bare essentials. A worn-out couch, a small kitchen table, and a single bed in the corner.

For a moment, Alexander stood in the middle of the room, taking it all in. This was his new reality, a world away from the life he had known. He felt the weight of the decision press down on him, the uncertainty of what lay ahead settling in his chest like a stone.

But there was no turning back now.

He placed his bag on the floor and sat down on the couch, leaning his head back against the wall. He closed his eyes for a moment, allowing himself a rare moment of peace.

It wasn't long before a knock on the door broke the silence. Alexander's heart raced in his chest, and for a brief second, he thought about abandoning the whole thing. But then, he remembered the choice he had made.

He stood and opened the door.

A woman stood in the hallway, a young woman with dark hair and a warm smile. She was holding a small basket of food—bread, eggs, and a few vegetables. Her eyes studied him for a moment, then softened.

"Hi," she said. "I'm your neighbor. I saw you moving in and thought I'd bring you some food. You know, to help you settle in."

Alexander was taken aback for a moment, unsure of how to respond. This wasn't the kind of gesture he was used to—gifts from assistants, business associates, people trying to ingratiate themselves with him. This was different. Genuine.

He managed a smile, trying to appear as ordinary as possible. "Thank you. That's very kind of you."

The woman nodded, handing him the basket. "No problem. I live just down the hall, if you need anything."

And just like that, she was gone, disappearing down the hallway, leaving Alexander standing in the doorway with the basket of food in his hands.

As he closed the door, he realized something—something he hadn't expected. In this world, the world of the "ordinary" people, kindness wasn't a currency that could be bought. It wasn't a transaction. It was a gift, freely given.

And it felt... unfamiliar.

The First Step

The first step had been taken. There was no going back now.

Three

A New Face

~~~

The apartment was cold, its bare walls offering no comfort to Alexander Moore as he stood in front of the small mirror above the bathroom sink. It wasn't much—just a cracked frame and a foggy reflection—but it was enough for him to see the transformation that had already begun.

His face was different now. Not in any drastic, physical way, but in the way his mind viewed it. The man he saw in the mirror no longer had the same confidence that had once radiated from him when he walked into a room. The reflection staring back at him was a stranger, someone who had yet to carve out his place in this new world. Gone was the meticulously groomed Alexander Moore—sharp, polished, flawless. In his place stood someone rougher, someone who had been worn down by life, someone who no longer belonged in the world he had left

A New Face

behind.

The door to the bathroom opened, and a voice echoed from the other room.

"Hey, you still alive in there?"

It was Emma—the woman who had knocked on his door the day before, offering him a basket of food, a gesture of kindness that had felt almost alien to him. He had barely caught her name before she disappeared down the hall. Now, here she was, a presence in his otherwise quiet, empty world.

He didn't respond immediately, staring at his reflection a little longer. He had to get used to this new face, this new life, but the adjustment was proving to be more difficult than he had imagined. It wasn't just about the clothes, the crumbling apartment, or the unfamiliar food he was eating. It was about everything—the constant reminder that he had given up everything, all for a fresh start.

"I'm here," he finally said, his voice rough from the unfamiliarity of the words. He had not yet fully found his new persona, and it made him feel exposed in ways he couldn't explain.

Emma's footsteps echoed down the hallway, and soon enough, she appeared in the doorway of the bathroom, her eyes studying him carefully. She was still wearing the same casual attire from the day before, jeans and a simple blouse, her dark hair pulled back into a loose ponytail. She had a quiet confidence about her, a grounded presence that made her stand out in a way

Alexander hadn't yet fully understood.

"Thought you might need some company," she said with a small, friendly smile. "I brought some more food—didn't know if you'd gotten enough last night."

Alexander couldn't help but notice how naturally kind she seemed. There was no ulterior motive, no hidden agenda. She simply wanted to make sure he wasn't struggling. And that was unsettling.

"I'm good, thanks," he replied, forcing a smile. "But, uh, I appreciate it."

She raised an eyebrow, studying him more intently now. Her eyes weren't judgmental, but there was something behind them that suggested she saw more than he wanted to reveal.

"How are you settling in?" she asked, her voice soft but insistent, as though she genuinely cared about his answer.

Alexander hesitated for a moment, unsure how to explain the disorientation he was feeling. There was a strange weight on his chest—a combination of isolation and uncertainty. The words didn't come easily to him. He wasn't used to this kind of vulnerability, and certainly not from someone like Emma, someone who had nothing to gain from his problems.

"I'm managing," he said, his voice betraying him slightly. He cleared his throat, trying to sound more convincing. "It's just... different, you know?"

A New Face

Emma stepped further into the room, placing the basket of food on the small table near the window. She looked at him, not with pity, but with understanding, as if she could sense his inner turmoil. "Yeah, I can imagine. But you'll get used to it. It's not so bad once you find your rhythm."

Her words seemed genuine, but there was a subtle undertone of curiosity in her voice. She wasn't just being kind; she was trying to understand him—maybe even figure out who he really was. Alexander felt the weight of that scrutiny, but he also felt a pull toward her. In this strange new world, she was the only constant he had.

"I hope so," he said, trying to shrug off the feeling that he was being analyzed. "How long have you lived here?"

Emma smiled, leaning against the counter as she began unpacking the basket. "Long enough. This place isn't much, but it's home. I've been here for about six months. Before that, I was in a different part of the city, but…" She trailed off, her eyes flickering to the floor for a moment before meeting his gaze again. "Life happens, right?"

Her voice was calm, but there was a depth in it that suggested she understood struggle in a way that Alexander wasn't used to. She wasn't talking about things he could relate to—corporate deals, investments, the kind of problems that consumed his former life. No, she was talking about real, raw life. The kind of life that made him feel like an outsider in his own skin.

"Yeah, life happens," he echoed, his voice distant, as he walked over to the window. He stood there for a long moment, his eyes scanning the street below. The world outside seemed so distant, so disconnected from the life he had once known.

"So, what's your story?" Emma's voice broke through the silence again. "You're not exactly from around here, are you?"

The question hit him like a jolt, and Alexander froze. He wasn't sure what to say. He had been careful to create a backstory for himself, a new identity that would allow him to blend in. But the truth was, he wasn't sure how much he wanted to share with her. Something about Emma's presence made him feel like he could trust her, but he knew better than to reveal too much. People in this world—this world he was now part of—couldn't be trusted with everything.

"I'm... just trying to get away from things," he said finally, turning his back on the window to face her. "I needed a change of scenery, you know?"

Emma seemed to buy it, her expression softening. "I get it. We all need a change sometimes. Everyone's got something they're running from."

Alexander felt a flicker of recognition at her words. It was the same in every life, wasn't it? Everyone was running from something, hiding from something. He certainly was. He just wasn't ready to confront whatever that thing was yet.

The silence between them stretched, thick with unspoken words. Alexander wasn't sure how much longer he could

A New Face

maintain this facade. He wasn't sure how much longer he could pretend to be someone he wasn't.

"You know," Emma said, breaking the silence once more, "if you ever need someone to talk to, I'm here. It's easy to feel lost when everything changes, but you're not alone."

Alexander's heart skipped a beat. It was such a simple offer, but it meant more than she could possibly know. He was used to being surrounded by people, but none of them had ever spoken to him like this—like he mattered, like he was worth something beyond his bank balance.

"Thanks," he said, his voice softer than he intended. "I appreciate that."

She nodded, standing up straight as if ready to leave. "Anyway, I'll let you get settled. But don't hesitate, okay? I'm just down the hall."

With that, she turned and walked toward the door, her footsteps light and unhurried. As she stepped into the hallway, she paused, looking back at him. "Take care of yourself, alright?"

"Yeah," Alexander replied, his voice barely a whisper. "You too."

As the door clicked shut behind her, Alexander stood in the middle of the small, sparse room, his mind racing. He wasn't sure what had just happened—whether he was beginning to understand the weight of this new life or whether he was losing himself in the process. But one thing was clear: Emma had given him something he hadn't expected—hope.

Hope that maybe, just maybe, he wasn't so alone in this world after all.

He reached up to the mirror again, staring at his reflection. The face looking back at him was still unfamiliar, still a stranger. But for the first time since stepping away from his former life, he didn't feel entirely lost.

This new face—this new identity—might just be the beginning of something real.

Four

Struggling to Fit In

The early morning light filtered through the thin curtains of Alexander's apartment, casting pale stripes across the floor. He had not slept well. The unfamiliar bed had offered no comfort, and his thoughts had been a whirlwind of confusion and doubt. He wasn't sure how he had gotten to this point, or what he was truly searching for. The luxury, the fame—it all seemed so far away now.

As he sat on the edge of the bed, staring at his reflection in the chipped mirror, the same question haunted him: Who am I now?

The noise of the city outside slowly began to rise, the hum of traffic, the chatter of pedestrians, the distant honking of horns—all of it unfamiliar, yet strangely comforting. This was his new world, a world where nothing mattered except survival and connection.

The clock on the wall ticked in the silence of the room, pulling him out of his reverie. He stood up and stretched, feeling the stiffness in his muscles from the restless night. Today was a new day. Today, he had to begin figuring out how to exist in this new life, this life that seemed so alien to him.

He had made the decision to leave behind his wealth, his status, his empire. Now, he was living in the shadows of his former self. But it wasn't just the material things that were slipping through his fingers—it was his identity.

It wasn't easy to fit into a world where you had nothing. Alexander had never known hardship. His upbringing had been one of privilege and protection, shielded from the realities that so many others faced. He had spent years in the world of high society, where success was measured in numbers and status, and where relationships were based on influence rather than sincerity. But now, he was in the heart of a poor, run-down neighborhood, surrounded by people who had struggled all their lives just to make ends meet.

He stood up, moved to the small kitchen, and poured himself a cup of coffee. The bitter, black liquid seemed to burn in his throat, but it was a necessary ritual, a moment of normalcy in a world that felt completely chaotic.

After drinking the coffee, he dressed quickly in the same worn clothes he had been wearing for the past couple of days—an old T-shirt and jeans. There was no mirror in the hallway, but he could feel the difference in his gait. He wasn't walking with the same confidence he had once exuded. He was trying to blend in, to disappear into the fabric of this new life, but it was harder than he expected. The air here felt thick with discomfort, and the constant reminder that he was playing a part, pretending to be someone he wasn't, gnawed at his insides.

He stepped out into the hallway, glancing at the door to the small apartment across from his. Emma had been kind to him, offering him food, offering him company. She had been his first real connection since stepping away from his former life, but there was something about her that unsettled him. She was too observant, too attuned to things that he wasn't ready to face.

As he stepped into the building's stairwell and began his descent toward the street, the noise of the outside world began to close in on him. He wasn't used to walking these streets, to the way the sound of footsteps and voices echoed through the cracked sidewalks. It was a world of rough edges and faded dreams, a world that didn't care about titles or fortunes.

At the corner of the street, a small grocery store sat, its windows dusty and its door hanging slightly off its hinges. Alexander hesitated, feeling a twinge of nervousness in his gut. He had never had to worry about what to buy in a store before. He had always had people to do that for him—assistants, chefs, personal shoppers. Now, he was on his own, and the realization was almost paralyzing. He wasn't sure what he was supposed to do, how to fit in. Was he supposed to pretend like this was easy? Or should he admit, even to himself, that he was struggling?

He pushed the door open and stepped inside. The store was cramped and smelled faintly of produce and old wood. Shelves lined with canned goods and stale bread greeted him. A woman stood behind the counter, her expression weary but kind. She looked up at him as he walked in, sizing him up quickly, her eyes sharp but not unfriendly.

"Can I help you with something?" she asked, her voice rough from years of speaking to customers.

Alexander opened his mouth but couldn't find the words. He wasn't sure what to ask for, or even how to ask for it. He felt out of place, like an imposter in a world that wasn't meant for him.

"Uh, yeah. Just… some bread and eggs," he said, trying to sound casual. But the words came out stiff, awkward, like he wasn't really sure what he needed.

The woman nodded and reached for the items, placing them on the counter with practiced ease. She didn't ask him any questions, didn't offer any small talk. In a way, that was a relief. The last thing he wanted was to draw attention to himself, to have anyone notice that he didn't belong.

He handed her a few crumpled bills, the only money he had on him. The woman glanced at the money briefly before taking it, and without another word, she handed him the items in a small paper bag.

"Here you go. Anything else?"

"No. That's it," Alexander said, eager to leave, to escape the discomfort of the moment. He took the bag and walked out of the store, trying not to look too out of place. The sound of his footsteps echoed in his ears as he made his way back to the apartment.

The walk back felt longer than it had any right to be. He wasn't used to this—this feeling of being lost in a world where he had no control, no power. Every corner he turned felt like another obstacle, another reminder of just how far he had fallen from the life he had known. He didn't belong here, not really. It was all so raw, so real, and yet he still couldn't shake the nagging feeling that he was an outsider in this new life.

When he finally reached the building, he went up the stairs slowly, the weight of his actions bearing down on him. Was this what he had wanted? To live like this? To give up everything that had once made him feel important? He wasn't sure anymore.

As he reached his door, he noticed a figure standing in the hallway—Emma. She was leaning against the wall, her arms crossed over her chest, looking at him with that same curious expression. Her presence made him uneasy, but he couldn't bring himself to look away.

"You okay?" she asked, her voice soft but insistent. "You've been gone for a while. Just wanted to make sure you're alright."

He nodded quickly, but his throat tightened. There was something about her concern that made him feel exposed, as if she could see right through him. She wasn't fooled by the act he was putting on. She could see the cracks in his armor, and it was both comforting and terrifying.

"Yeah, just needed to get some things," he said, forcing a smile. "Thanks for checking on me."

She didn't say anything at first, just watched him, her eyes thoughtful. Finally, she spoke again.

"You know, you don't have to do this alone," she said, her voice low. "I get that you're... adjusting. But you don't have to hide it. If you need help, if you need to talk, I'm here."

Alexander felt a lump rise in his throat. He didn't know how to respond. He wanted to tell her everything, to explain the pressure he was under, the constant battle between the life he had left and the person he was trying to become. But he couldn't. Not yet.

Instead, he just nodded and mumbled, "Thanks, Emma."

She gave him a small smile before turning and walking back to her apartment, leaving him standing in the hallway alone.

As he closed his door behind him, the weight of the day settled in. He was struggling to fit in, to make this new life work. It was harder than he had ever imagined, and with every passing moment, it felt like he was losing more of himself.

But there was no turning back. He had made this choice, and now he had to live with it.

Struggling to Fit In

The question lingered in the air as he sank into the worn-out couch—how long would it take before the world he had left behind caught up with him?

Five

Emma's Secret

The evening air was thick with humidity, and the dim glow of streetlights flickered in the distance, casting long shadows down the narrow alleyways of the neighborhood. Alexander stood on his balcony, looking out over the city, a city that felt so different now. He could still see the skyline—the high-rise buildings, the shimmering lights, the distant hum of activity—but everything about it now felt distant, disconnected. The world he had once commanded seemed like it belonged to someone else, someone far removed from the man who stood on the edge of his balcony, lost in his thoughts.

He had tried to push the nagging feeling of regret away, but it clung to him like a shadow. What was he doing here? What was he hoping to find? He had abandoned everything—his fortune, his title, his future—just to live in this gritty neighborhood, surrounded by people who had lived their entire lives in struggle. And for what? To escape a life that now felt meaningless? Or was he simply running from something deeper, something that he couldn't yet name?

A soft knock on his door startled him, and for a moment, he considered ignoring it. He didn't feel like company—not tonight. But then the thought of Emma crossed his mind, and the faint echo of her kindness and understanding made him open the door.

Standing in the hallway was Emma, her dark hair pulled back into a loose bun, wearing a simple, faded T-shirt and jeans. She wasn't carrying anything this time, but there was a warmth in her eyes that made her seem familiar, almost like someone he could trust. But he couldn't afford to trust anyone—not here, not now. Not even her.

"Hey," she greeted, offering him a hesitant smile. "You busy?"

He stepped aside to let her in, his eyes narrowing slightly as he tried to gauge her intentions. There was something different about her today—something subtle, but unmistakable. She seemed more guarded than usual, as though she was holding something back. For a moment, he considered asking her about it, but the words never came. He didn't want to risk exposing himself, not when he still hadn't figured out what he was doing here.

"Not really," he said, trying to keep his tone casual as he motioned for her to sit. "What's up?"

Emma walked in, glancing around the sparse apartment before sitting down on the couch. She didn't immediately speak, her eyes flitting to the worn furniture, the bare walls, the lack of decoration. It was as if she was taking in everything about his new life, silently measuring it.

"I've been meaning to talk to you," she finally said, her voice hesitant, but resolute. "About... about something."

Alexander froze. The air between them seemed to thicken, and he immediately felt the hairs on the back of his neck stand on end. He had known this was coming. The questions, the probing, the curiosity. She had noticed his strange behavior, his sudden disappearance from the life he had led before, and now she wanted answers.

"What about?" he asked, his voice calm but tight with tension. He leaned against the doorframe, crossing his arms over his chest as if to shield himself from whatever she was about to reveal.

Emma hesitated, her gaze flickering to the floor before meeting his eyes. "I know you've been hiding something," she said softly. "I don't know what it is, but I can tell. You're not... you're not just some guy looking for a fresh start. There's something else. Something you're running from."

For a moment, Alexander said nothing. The weight of her words sank into him, pressing against his chest like an invisible hand. She was right—he wasn't just running from the life he had left behind. He was running from something far deeper, something more painful than he was willing to admit, even to himself. But he couldn't tell her that—not yet.

"I'm just trying to figure things out," he finally said, his voice low, his eyes avoiding hers. "I told you, I needed a change."

Emma watched him for a moment, her eyes unreadable. "It's not just a change, though, is it? You're hiding something. And I think... I think you've been through something. Something that's still eating at you. I want to help you, Alexander. But I can't if you don't trust me."

The way she said his name made his heart skip a beat. There was something in her voice, something that softened the edges of his defenses. But he couldn't—he couldn't tell her the truth. Not yet.

Before he could respond, Emma stood up abruptly, her expression shifting. "Maybe I'm wrong. Maybe I've just been imagining things. Maybe you really are just a guy trying to escape. But I can't just stand by and pretend like I don't see what's happening."

She turned toward the door, and for a brief moment, Alexander thought she was going to leave. But then she stopped, her hand resting on the doorknob, her back still turned to him.

"You want to know something?" she said, her voice barely above a whisper. "I'm not who I say I am, either."

The words hit Alexander like a punch to the gut. He felt the ground beneath him shift, the room spinning as his mind raced to process what she had just said.

"What do you mean?" he asked, his voice betraying his shock. "What are you talking about?"

Emma slowly turned around, her face serious now, her eyes darkened with something deeper—something more dangerous.

"I'm not just some waitress trying to make ends meet," she said, her voice steady, but with a hint of vulnerability beneath the surface. "I didn't grow up here. I didn't… I didn't choose this life. It was thrust upon me. And I've been running from my past just like you've been running from yours."

Alexander stood there, his mouth suddenly dry. His mind raced, but the words wouldn't come. He hadn't expected this—he hadn't expected her to reveal her own secret, her own story. It was too much. The walls around him, the ones he had spent so much time building up, were beginning to crumble.

"What are you hiding?" he asked, his voice barely above a whisper. "Why didn't you tell me?"

Emma stepped closer, her eyes searching his face. She seemed to be weighing whether to continue, whether to let him in on whatever it was that had shaped her into the person standing before him now. Her lips parted, as if she were about to speak, but instead, she sighed deeply, a sound of weariness, of acceptance.

Emma's Secret

"I can't tell you everything," she said softly, "not yet. But I will. Just... not right now."

Alexander could see the weight of her words, the struggle within her. He wanted to push her for more, to demand answers, but he knew she wasn't ready to give them. And for some reason, he found himself understanding that. They were both hiding, both running from things that could destroy them if revealed.

For a long time, neither of them spoke. The silence in the room was thick with unsaid words, with secrets that neither of them were ready to expose. But in that moment, something changed. They were no longer just two strangers pretending to be something they weren't. They were two people, wounded and searching for something real, something that might just exist between the cracks of their carefully constructed lies.

Finally, Emma turned and walked toward the door. "I'll tell you when I'm ready," she said, her voice low but firm. "But you have to promise me something, Alexander."

"What?"

"Don't hide from me. Not anymore. We're both here for a reason. We both need to figure things out. And we can't do that if we keep pretending like everything's fine."

Alexander stood there, watching her, his heart pounding in his chest. For the first time since he had arrived in this strange new world, he felt like he wasn't alone.

"I promise," he said quietly, though he wasn't sure if he believed it himself.

Emma gave him a small nod before stepping out into the hallway, closing the door behind her. As he stood there, alone in the dimly lit room, Alexander felt the weight of her words settle into his bones.

They were both running from something. And sooner or later, the truth was going to catch up with them both.

Six

A Moment of Weakness

The apartment was eerily quiet, save for the faint hum of the refrigerator and the occasional creak of the building's aging infrastructure. Alexander sat on the edge of the couch, his hands resting on his knees, staring at the walls as though they could offer him some kind of answer. He had been in the same position for hours, his mind racing, the same thoughts swirling over and over again. He couldn't seem to shake them.

Emma's words still lingered in the air, heavy and unspoken, pressing against him. Don't hide from me. Not anymore. He had promised, and he meant it, but how could he face the truth? How could he expose the rawness of his feelings, the vulnerability that came with revealing the reasons for his escape, the reasons he had abandoned everything he had once known?

The weight of his decision to leave his old life behind had been suffocating, but now, it was the uncertainty of his future that was crushing him. He was caught between two worlds—the world he had built, filled with luxury and influence, and the world he was now living in, where survival mattered more than status. He had come here looking for something real, something untarnished by the mask of wealth, but the harder he tried to immerse himself in this new reality, the more it felt like he was playing a role he wasn't meant to.

A knock on the door startled him from his thoughts. His heart skipped a beat, and he immediately stood, feeling an odd sense of dread wash over him. He didn't know who it could be. The landlord? A neighbor? Or someone from his past who had somehow found him?

He hesitated for a moment before walking toward the door. His hands felt clammy as he reached for the handle. For the first time since his arrival, he wasn't sure he was ready to face anyone. But he couldn't ignore the knock. Not now.

He opened the door, his breath catching when he saw Emma standing in the hallway. She looked different today—her hair was down, her face more solemn than usual. She didn't have the same warmth in her eyes, and for a fleeting moment, Alexander wondered if something had shifted between them. Maybe she had seen through the cracks in his carefully constructed life. Maybe she knew that the man he had presented himself to be was nothing more than a facade.

"Hey," she said, her voice softer than usual. "Can we talk?"

A Moment of Weakness

The words hung in the air between them, and for a moment, Alexander didn't know what to say. He had been avoiding this—avoiding her—because he didn't know how to explain himself. He didn't know how to tell her that he was still trying to figure out who he was, still lost in the maze of his own identity. But here she was, standing in front of him, her eyes searching his, as if waiting for him to reveal something he wasn't ready to give.

"Sure," he replied, stepping aside to let her in.

Emma walked past him, her footsteps light but deliberate. She seemed more subdued today, her usual energy replaced with an air of quiet tension. She didn't immediately sit down but instead moved to the window, staring out at the city below. The same city he had once ruled, the same city that now felt so distant.

"I've been thinking," she began, her voice almost too calm, too controlled. "About everything. About you. About me. And I don't think I can keep pretending like I don't see what's really going on."

Alexander swallowed hard. His pulse quickened. He knew what was coming, and yet he couldn't bring himself to stop it. He had tried to shut it out, to bury it deep inside, but the truth had a way of clawing its way to the surface, no matter how hard he tried to ignore it.

"I don't know what you mean," he said, his voice betraying him slightly. The words felt hollow, meaningless in the face of her gaze.

Emma turned to face him, her expression unreadable. There was something in her eyes—something raw and vulnerable—that made his heart ache. It was as if she had peeled back the layers of his facade and saw him for who he really was, and it terrified him.

"I mean that you're not who you say you are, Alexander," she said quietly. "And I'm not either. I've been pretending too. We've both been pretending. And I think we both know it."

The words hit him like a physical blow. He opened his mouth to protest, to deny it, but no words came. He had spent so much time running from the truth that he didn't even know how to face it anymore. But Emma, with her quiet strength, had cut through the layers he had carefully built up. She had seen past the lies and had found the man underneath—the man who was still trying to find his way.

"I didn't choose this life," she continued, her voice steady despite the vulnerability in her eyes. "I didn't choose to be here, to be stuck in this... this rut. But here I am. And you're here too, pretending like you're just some guy trying to start over. But I know better. I know that's not the real reason."

Alexander's breath caught in his throat. He didn't want to hear this. He didn't want to admit that she was right. But deep down, he knew she was. He wasn't here just because he wanted to escape. He wasn't here just to find something real. He was here because he had lost everything, and he was running from the consequences of his choices.

A Moment of Weakness

But there was more to it than that. There had to be. He wasn't just hiding from his past—he was hiding from himself. He was afraid of confronting the man he had become, the man who had let ambition, power, and money consume him.

He took a step toward her, his voice shaking as he spoke. "What do you want from me, Emma? What do you expect me to say?"

Emma's gaze softened, and for the first time, Alexander saw something that he hadn't expected—compassion. She wasn't judging him. She wasn't angry with him. She was simply trying to understand.

"I'm not asking you to say anything," she said quietly. "I'm asking you to be real. With me. With yourself. I've told you I'm here for you, and I mean it. But I can't help you if you're not willing to face what's really going on."

The words hung in the air between them, suspended in a moment of perfect tension. Alexander felt a surge of frustration welling up inside him. He wanted to lash out, to tell her that she didn't know what he had been through, that she couldn't possibly understand the weight of the life he had lived. But he didn't say any of that. Instead, he felt something else—a rawness, a vulnerability he had been avoiding for so long.

For the first time since he had come to this apartment, he felt a crack in his armor. He could no longer hide behind the walls he had built around himself. He was tired. So damn tired. Tired of pretending, tired of running, tired of trying to be someone he wasn't.

Without warning, the words spilled out of him, raw and unfiltered.

"I don't know who I am anymore, Emma," he said, his voice breaking. "I thought I was running from my past, from my wealth, from everything I've built. But the truth is, I'm running from myself. I don't know how to be the person I want to be. I don't know how to face the things I've done, the choices I've made. And I'm scared. Scared that if I let go of everything, I won't be anyone at all."

Emma stood still, her eyes never leaving him. For a moment, there was nothing but the sound of his ragged breathing, and the weight of his confession seemed to hang in the air, heavier than anything he had ever carried before.

And then, she took a step toward him, her presence grounding him in a way he hadn't expected. She reached out, her hand brushing against his arm, her touch gentle but firm.

"You're not alone," she said softly. "You don't have to do this alone."

The words, simple yet powerful, cut through the fog of his confusion. For the first time in what felt like forever, Alexander felt something shift inside him. He wasn't sure if it was hope, or something else entirely, but it was enough to make him believe that maybe—just maybe—he wasn't beyond saving.

A moment of weakness. A crack in the armor. And for the first time, he wasn't afraid to let it in.

A Moment of Weakness

He looked at Emma, and for the first time since he had met her, he saw her not as a stranger, but as someone who understood. And in that moment, something changed.

He wasn't running anymore.

Not from her. Not from himself.

Seven

Dangerous Consequences

The sun had already begun to dip below the horizon, casting an orange hue across the sky that felt surreal, almost out of place. Alexander stood on the rooftop of his building, staring out at the sprawling city below. It was the city that had once been his kingdom, a place where his decisions shaped industries, where his wealth commanded respect. But now, it felt alien to him—distant and unreachable, like a dream he could no longer grasp.

He had done it. He had made the decision to walk away from everything, to start over in a life that seemed far removed from the one he had once known. But the weight of his choice pressed down on him more heavily each day. As much as he wanted to embrace this new life, to leave behind the persona of Alexander Moore, billionaire CEO, the consequences were catching up to him.

His thoughts were interrupted by the sound of footsteps behind him. He turned, his heart skipping a beat as he saw Emma emerge from the stairwell. She looked tired—her hair slightly disheveled, her face drawn—but there was a determination in her eyes that Alexander had come to recognize. She had been a constant in his life since he arrived, a presence that grounded him, even as the world around him seemed to spin out of control. But now, her expression was different. There was an edge to it, something that made the hairs on the back of his neck stand up.

"I need to talk to you," Emma said, her voice steady but laced with an urgency that made Alexander's pulse quicken. She didn't wait for a response, simply walking toward him and stopping a few feet away, her gaze fixed on him.

Alexander didn't speak, but his heart began to race. Something was wrong. He could feel it in the air between them, a tension that was almost suffocating. He had seen Emma face hardship, had seen her struggle in ways he could barely comprehend, but this was different. This was a warning. He could sense it.

"What's going on?" he asked, his voice strained. He wanted to know, but at the same time, he wasn't sure if he was ready to hear it.

Emma exhaled sharply, her shoulders sagging slightly as if the weight of what she was about to say was almost too much to bear. She looked at him, her eyes searching his face as though trying to gauge his reaction before she spoke. "I found something," she began slowly, "something that's going to change everything. Something that I should have told you earlier."

The words hit him like a punch to the gut. "What are you talking about?" Alexander's voice was barely a whisper, his body tense as he braced for the inevitable.

Emma took a step closer, lowering her voice. "I've been trying to keep this from you, but I can't anymore. I thought I could protect you from the consequences of your past, but I've realized now that I'm just as tangled in this as you are. There are people—dangerous people—who know who you really are."

The words echoed in his mind as the world around him seemed to blur. Dangerous people? Alexander felt his breath catch in his throat. He had been living in constant fear that his old life would come crashing back into this new, fragile existence he was building. But hearing Emma say it aloud, hearing the fear in her voice, made it feel all too real.

"Who are they?" he demanded, his hands clenched into fists as he stepped closer to her. "What do you know?"

Emma hesitated for a moment, and for the briefest second, Alexander saw something flicker in her eyes—a shadow of fear that she was desperately trying to hide. She opened her mouth to speak, but before she could, the sound of a car engine revving loudly echoed from below, followed by the screech of tires on the pavement.

Without thinking, Alexander turned toward the edge of the rooftop, his eyes scanning the streets below. The streetlights flickered on, casting an eerie glow on the scene unfolding in front of him. There, on the corner of the street, was a black SUV parked haphazardly, its engine still roaring as a group of men emerged from the vehicle. They wore dark suits, their faces obscured by the shadows, but there was no mistaking the menacing energy that surrounded them.

Emma stepped back, her eyes widening in fear as she glanced between the men and Alexander. "They're here," she whispered, her voice trembling. "They know you're here. They found you."

For a moment, everything seemed to freeze. Alexander's heart pounded in his chest as he turned back to Emma, his mind racing. How did they find me? he thought. I've been so careful. I've done everything right.

But it didn't matter now. The past had finally caught up with him, and the consequences of his actions were about to unfold in a way he couldn't control.

"We need to leave," Emma said, her voice urgent now as she grabbed his arm. "They'll come for us if we stay here. We can't—"

Before she could finish, there was a loud crash from the stairwell below, followed by heavy footsteps. The door to the rooftop swung open with a deafening bang, and two men in black suits appeared, their eyes locked on Alexander. One of them had a scar running down his cheek, the other a cold, calculating expression that sent a chill down Alexander's spine.

"Mr. Moore," the man with the scar said, his voice low and dangerous. "It's time to come with us."

Emma stepped in front of Alexander, blocking the men with her body. "You're not taking him," she said, her voice steady, though her eyes betrayed the fear she was trying to hide. "You have no right to—"

"Step aside," the man growled, taking a step toward her. "You don't want to get in our way."

Alexander's mind raced as he tried to process what was happening. These men—who were they? How did they know where he was? What did they want with him?

Before he could think any further, the man with the scar raised his hand, signaling to the other man. Without warning, the second man lunged at Emma, grabbing her by the wrist and pulling her out of the way. Emma fought back, but her strength was no match for the man's grip.

"Let her go!" Alexander shouted, his heart pounding in his chest. He stepped forward, only to be met with the cold gaze of the man with the scar.

"You're coming with us, Moore," the man said, his tone final. "No more running."

Alexander's blood ran cold as the weight of the situation sank in. These men were no ordinary thugs. They were professionals. And they weren't here to ask questions—they were here to deliver a message.

"I'm not going anywhere," Alexander said, his voice growing louder, more desperate. "I'm not the man you think I am."

The man with the scar didn't even flinch. "You're wrong about that, Moore," he said. "You're exactly the man we thought you were. And you've made a lot of people very angry."

Before Alexander could respond, the man raised his hand, signaling to his partner. In an instant, the other man reached into his jacket and pulled out a gun. The cold metal gleamed in the dim light, and Alexander's heart skipped a beat as he felt the weight of the situation settle over him.

"Move," the man with the scar ordered.

Emma struggled in the other man's grip, but it was futile. She was outnumbered, and her resistance only seemed to anger them more.

"Don't," Alexander said, his voice thick with fear. He couldn't let them take Emma. He couldn't let them drag her into whatever mess he had gotten himself into.

But the gun was still pointed at him, and the reality of the situation hit him like a freight train. He was cornered. There was no escape. No way out.

The men took another step forward, their faces cold, indifferent to the chaos around them.

And then, in the distance, a voice broke through the tension.

"Enough!"

The command came from across the rooftop, and Alexander's eyes snapped toward the source. A figure stepped out from the shadows, his silhouette tall and imposing. The man's face was obscured by the low light, but there was no mistaking the authority in his voice.

The two men in black suits froze, their eyes darting toward the newcomer.

"You have your orders," the man said, his voice carrying a dangerous edge. "But I'm the one who calls the shots now."

The standoff between the two groups was electric, charged with a tension so thick it felt like the air itself was holding its breath.

For the first time since the men had arrived, Alexander felt a sliver of hope. But it was fleeting, like a flicker of light in a storm.

He didn't know who this new man was, but he knew one thing for sure—his dangerous consequences had only just begun.

Eight

The Unraveling

~~~

The air was thick with tension, the rooftop feeling more like a battleground than a place of refuge. Alexander could feel the weight of the situation pressing down on him, as though the ground beneath his feet had shifted, and he was standing on unstable ground. The men in black suits—those who had come for him—now stood frozen, their eyes locked on the man who had stepped out of the shadows. He was tall, his posture rigid and commanding, but there was something unsettling about the way he moved, like a predator circling its prey.

For a moment, the world seemed to hold its breath.

"Who are you?" one of the men with the scar growled, his voice betraying a mixture of confusion and suspicion. He didn't lower his weapon, but there was a hesitation in his stance, a moment of uncertainty that hadn't been there before.

The tall figure—who was now revealed to be a man of imposing stature and cold eyes—moved forward, his steps slow and deliberate. There was no rush, no urgency in his movements, but everything about him exuded power. He stopped a few feet away from the men, his gaze cold as he assessed them with a clinical detachment.

"I think you're in the wrong place," the man said, his voice smooth, almost too calm. His eyes flickered to Alexander and then back to the men. "But I'm not here to argue. I'm here to give you a choice."

The tension between the two sides could be cut with a knife. Alexander felt his breath catch in his throat. A choice? What kind of choice? And who was this man?

The men with the guns exchanged uneasy glances, clearly taken aback by the newcomer's casual yet authoritative demeanor. The one with the scar gritted his teeth, his grip tightening on the weapon.

"We don't take orders from strangers," he spat, taking a half step forward, as if daring the man to make a move. "You've got no business here."

The man in the shadows smiled, the expression cold, devoid of warmth. "I'm not a stranger to you, not anymore." His eyes flickered briefly to Emma, still struggling in the grip of the other man. "And as for your business, well, that's where it gets interesting."

Before Alexander could make sense of the situation, the man continued, his tone now turning sharper, more dangerous.

"Let her go," the newcomer ordered. The command was simple, but it carried a weight that none of them could ignore.

The man holding Emma hesitated, his grip loosening for a fraction of a second, but just long enough for her to twist away. She broke free, stumbling backward toward Alexander. The moment she was clear, the man with the scar gestured sharply to his partner.

"Get her back," he barked.

But the newcomer didn't move. His eyes, still locked on the two men, seemed to measure their every move, as though he were anticipating their next action.

"Enough of this," the stranger said, his voice now laced with a dangerous calm that made the air feel even heavier. "You've been given your chance. Leave. Now."

The men stood still for a long moment, the only sound being the distant rumble of the city beneath them. Finally, the man with the scar made a sharp motion toward the SUV. "This isn't over," he said, his voice low, filled with menace. "You can't hide forever, Moore."

As the two men turned and retreated, disappearing down the

stairs, the weight of the encounter settled heavily in the air. Alexander's heart was still racing, his breath coming in shallow gasps. He didn't know who this man was or why he had intervened, but the reality of the moment was undeniable: they had narrowly escaped danger.

Emma was still standing a few feet away, her chest heaving with quick breaths. She looked at Alexander, her eyes wide with a mixture of relief and confusion. "Who was that?" she whispered.

Alexander couldn't answer. The stranger's words echoed in his mind: You've been given your chance. Leave. Now. But leave? Where could they go? What kind of world had they just entered?

He glanced toward the stairwell, but the men with the guns were already gone. For a moment, he felt a strange sense of calm wash over him, but it was quickly replaced by a deeper fear—the kind that gripped his insides like a vice.

"What's happening, Emma?" His voice was strained, desperate. "Who were those men? Why are they after me?"

Emma didn't immediately answer. She was still staring at the spot where the men had disappeared, her face pale, her mind clearly working through the same questions.

The man who had intervened had been the only person who seemed in control of the situation. The only one who seemed to have the power to defuse the situation, to turn the tables. But

The Unraveling

who was he? And why had he come for them?

"I don't know," Emma said finally, her voice shaking. "But we have to get out of here. Those men… they weren't just anyone. They knew who you were, Alexander. They weren't here to negotiate—they were here to take you. And if they come back, we won't be able to stop them again."

Alexander's mind was spinning. The life he had tried to leave behind, the world he had hoped to escape, had just come crashing into this quiet, fragile existence. These men, whoever they were, had found him. And it wasn't just about his past anymore. It was about his future. About Emma. About everything he had tried to protect.

The man who had intervened—he wasn't just a stranger. He was someone with power, someone who seemed to know more about Alexander's past than he did himself.

"Who are you?" Alexander demanded, spinning to face the figure who had saved them. "What do you want?"

The stranger stepped forward, his presence imposing, though there was no sign of the violent energy that had surrounded the other men. His eyes locked onto Alexander's, calculating and cold.

"You don't remember me, do you?" the man said, his voice laced with a bitterness that Alexander couldn't quite place. "It's been a long time."

Alexander's heart skipped a beat. A long time? What did that mean? The man's face was sharp, his jaw tight, but Alexander didn't recognize him. His mind raced, trying to place the face, but the more he tried, the less he remembered.

"You've been running, Alexander," the stranger continued, his voice edged with anger. "Hiding from the life you built. But the thing about running is that it always catches up to you."

The words hit Alexander like a blow to the chest. It was as though the stranger had peeled back a layer of his soul, revealing the raw truth he had been too afraid to face. He had been running. Running from his wealth, running from the consequences of his actions, running from everything that had defined him.

The stranger's eyes narrowed. "You think you can just leave all of that behind? That you can walk away from the people you've wronged and live some quiet life? You can't, Moore. Not anymore."

Alexander took a step back, his chest tightening as the weight of the stranger's words sank in. "What do you want from me?" he demanded again, his voice hoarse.

The stranger's lips curled into a bitter smile. "What I want doesn't matter anymore," he said. "But you should know this: the people you've crossed—they don't forget. And they don't forgive."

Emma took a step closer to Alexander, her face tense with fear.

The Unraveling

She could sense the unraveling of something much larger than the two of them, something that was spiraling out of control. And she wasn't sure how much longer they could keep running.

"I'll tell you everything," the stranger said suddenly, his voice lowering to a dangerous whisper. "But not here. Not now."

Before either Alexander or Emma could respond, the man turned and walked toward the stairwell, his movements swift and purposeful. He didn't look back, but his presence left an undeniable weight in the air.

"We need to go," Emma said urgently, her eyes wide with fear. "We don't have time."

Alexander didn't need any more convincing. He had already seen the dangers that had been lurking at the edges of his life, waiting to consume him. And now, as the stranger's cryptic words echoed in his mind, he understood one thing: he couldn't outrun the past. It was already too late.

The unraveling had begun.

Nine

The Wade

The night had settled heavily over the city, casting shadows that seemed to stretch on forever. Alexander walked quickly, his mind spinning with the words of the stranger. You think you can just leave all of that behind? The words echoed in his ears, a bitter reminder of the life he had tried to escape, only to realize that no matter how far he ran, it would always catch up with him.

Emma walked beside him, her steps quick but her eyes constantly darting around, scanning the darkened streets as though expecting something—someone—to appear at any moment. The fear in her expression matched the tension in his chest. The city, which had once felt like a maze of opportunities, now felt like a trap closing in on him.

"Where are we going?" Emma's voice broke through the silence, her tone sharp with urgency.

Alexander didn't know. He had no real plan. After the stranger's cryptic warning, after the encounter with the men in black suits, he felt more lost than ever. Every decision he had made since arriving in this neighborhood—since leaving everything behind—seemed like the wrong one.

"We need to get out of here," he said, his voice low, his mind racing. "I don't know where, but we can't stay here. Not anymore."

Emma didn't respond immediately, but her eyes narrowed as she looked at him, trying to read his face. She had always been able to read people, to sense when something was off. And she could tell that Alexander was on the verge of something—something big. Something that could change everything.

They turned down an alleyway, away from the main streets, and the darkness seemed to close in around them. The streetlights above flickered, casting long, eerie shadows across the cracked pavement. Alexander's heart raced as they moved further into the maze of narrow streets, his mind still swirling with questions. Who was that man? And what did he mean when he said that the people Alexander had crossed didn't forget or forgive?

They had made it to the end of the alley when a voice from behind them stopped them cold.

"Where do you think you're going?"

It was the same voice—the one that had haunted Alexander's thoughts all night. The stranger. The man who had come to his rescue, only to drop a bombshell that had turned everything upside down.

Alexander spun around, his breath catching in his throat as he saw the figure standing in the shadows, illuminated only by the dim light of the streetlamp behind him. The man's face was still hard to read, but there was something colder in his eyes now, something more dangerous.

"I told you before," the man said, his voice low, almost amused. "You can't hide from this."

Emma stepped forward, her fists clenched, ready to defend herself—and Alexander—but the stranger simply held up a hand, signaling her to stop. She hesitated, eyes narrowing as she studied the man, but she didn't make a move.

"You're making a mistake," Alexander said, trying to steady his breathing, trying to think clearly. "I'm not the man you think I am. I'm not part of whatever it is you're accusing me of."

The man let out a soft, humorless chuckle. "You really don't remember, do you?" he asked, almost pityingly. "You've been running for so long, trying to bury the truth, but you can't outrun it forever, Moore."

"Who are you?" Alexander demanded, stepping closer, his fists clenched at his sides. "What do you want from me?"

The Wade

The stranger didn't answer immediately. Instead, he glanced over at Emma, studying her with an intensity that sent a shiver down Alexander's spine. The man's eyes flickered to her wrist—where a faint mark of a scar seemed to linger—and then back to Alexander.

"We're not here to hurt you," the stranger said, his voice dropping slightly. "We're here to make you understand. To make you see what you've done."

Alexander's stomach twisted. Something about the way the man spoke, about the way he looked at Emma, made everything inside of him flare with a sense of dread. He didn't know what the man meant, but he had a feeling it was something far worse than anything he could imagine.

"What do you mean, what I've done?" Alexander asked, his voice quieter now, betraying the growing fear inside of him.

"You've crossed the wrong people, Moore," the stranger said, his eyes narrowing. "Your wealth, your company, your position—it's all just a mask. A mask that hid what you really are. What you really did."

Emma stepped forward then, her voice low, but strong. "You're lying. Whatever it is you think he's done, you've got it all wrong."

The man's eyes flickered to her once more, and for a moment, Alexander saw a flash of something—recognition? Hatred? He couldn't be sure. But the look was enough to make his blood run cold.

"You're more involved in this than you think," the man said, his voice deadly quiet. "You both are. It's not just Alexander's past that's at stake here. It's yours too."

The words felt like a blow to Alexander's chest. What was he talking about? What did he mean? Had Emma been hiding something? He turned to her, searching her face, trying to understand what was happening.

"Emma," he said, his voice tight. "What is he talking about? What does he mean?"

Emma's face paled, her lips pressing together into a thin line. She looked away from him, her eyes flickering to the man in the shadows, before turning back to Alexander. The silence between them stretched on, thick and suffocating.

"I don't know," she said finally, her voice barely above a whisper. "I don't know what he's talking about, but you have to believe me, Alexander. I'm not part of this."

But there was something in her eyes—a flicker of uncertainty—that made Alexander's stomach twist. She was hiding something, he could feel it. And that something was more dangerous than either of them could have imagined.

The man in the shadows let out a low sigh. "I warned you both. You've been running from the wrong thing, and now, it's too late." He stepped forward, his hand reaching into his jacket, pulling out a small device. It was black, sleek, and with a few quick movements, he pressed a button.

A soft beep filled the air, and for a moment, everything went still.

"What's happening?" Alexander asked, his heart pounding as he watched the man closely.

The stranger didn't answer right away. He simply stared at the device, his face betraying no emotion, before looking up at Alexander and Emma with a chilling smile. "You've been on borrowed time. And now the clock's running out."

A sharp, shrill sound pierced the quiet night, and Alexander's blood ran cold. It was the sound of an alarm, faint at first, but growing louder. The man's eyes locked onto Alexander's, as if daring him to react.

"Time's up," the stranger said with an air of finality.

Before either Alexander or Emma could make sense of what was happening, a group of men appeared from the shadows, emerging quickly from the alleyway. Their movements were coordinated, precise. The men had the same cold, calculating look that the stranger had, and Alexander could see that they were all armed. Their presence confirmed one thing: the danger was real. This wasn't a bluff. This was a trap that was closing in on him from all sides.

"Run!" Emma shouted, grabbing Alexander's arm and pulling

him toward the alleyway, away from the oncoming men.

But they were too late. The men had already begun to surround them, cutting off every escape route. Alexander felt a surge of panic rise in his chest as the walls seemed to close in. His mind raced, but there were no options left. They were trapped.

The stranger stepped forward, his hands held up in mock surrender. "There's nowhere to run, Moore. You're not leaving here without answering for what you've done."

As the men closed in around them, Alexander's thoughts scrambled. He didn't know what was happening. He didn't know what he had done. But he knew one thing: the unraveling had started. And now, there was no escaping the consequences.

The past was catching up with him. And this time, there was no hiding.

Ten

A Reckoning

The air was thick with tension, the city's distant hum muffled by the suffocating atmosphere in the alley. Alexander's chest was tight, his breath coming in short, rapid bursts. His mind raced, struggling to piece together the fragments of reality that had begun to splinter around him. The men in black suits, the stranger's cryptic words, and now Emma, who was standing beside him, her face a mixture of fear and determination.

They were trapped.

Surrounded by figures whose expressions were unreadable, their eyes cold and unyielding. There was no escape. No way out.

"What is this?" Alexander finally managed to ask, his voice

hoarse, but still full of defiance. He stepped forward, trying to steady himself despite the mounting anxiety clawing at his chest. "What do you want from me?"

The stranger, who had been the one to pull the strings behind this sudden onslaught, stepped closer. His tall frame seemed to fill the alleyway, his presence commanding attention. There was an unsettling calmness to his demeanor, as if he had already won. His cold eyes didn't leave Alexander's face.

"You still don't get it, do you?" The stranger's voice was low, almost like a whisper, but it carried a dangerous edge. "You think you can just run away, live some quiet life, and erase everything you've done. But you can't, Alexander. You've made your choices, and now it's time to face them."

Emma moved slightly in front of Alexander, her stance protective, but her hands were trembling. She had been quiet ever since the stranger had appeared, her expression unreadable, but her eyes betrayed a flicker of something—regret, perhaps. Fear. Alexander's pulse quickened as he turned to her.

"Emma," he said, his voice tight with a mix of confusion and desperation. "What's going on? What do you know?"

Emma didn't immediately respond. Instead, she kept her gaze fixed on the stranger, as though calculating something, weighing her options. When she finally spoke, her voice was barely above a whisper.

"I didn't want you to know," she said, her eyes shifting to

A Reckoning

Alexander's. "But you deserve the truth."

The words hung in the air between them, thick and heavy. Alexander's heart skipped a beat, his mind struggling to catch up with the growing dread in his chest. What truth? What was she hiding?

The stranger stepped closer, his eyes narrowing as he took in the exchange. "She's not the only one with secrets, Moore. You've spent years running from yours. Hiding behind your wealth, your status. But no one escapes forever."

Alexander felt a rush of panic surge through him. The reality of the situation was settling in—this wasn't just some misguided attack. This was about power. This was about the life he had left behind, and now, it was coming back with a vengeance. And Emma—Emma, who had seemed like his lifeline in this chaotic world—was wrapped up in it too.

"I don't understand," Alexander said, his voice a mix of frustration and disbelief. "I left everything behind. I'm not the same man anymore. I'm not—"

"Not the same man?" The stranger laughed, a sharp, humorless sound that sent a shiver down Alexander's spine. "You think you can change that easily? You think you can just erase the past with a few actions? You can't. Your sins have caught up with you, Moore. And now, you have to pay the price."

There was a cold finality in the stranger's voice that sent chills through Alexander's body. His knees felt weak, and his pulse pounded in his ears. He had known the danger was always there, lurking in the corners of his mind, but this—this feeling of inevitability—it was suffocating.

Emma took a deep breath, her eyes flickering between Alexander and the stranger. "I never wanted you to get involved in this," she said, her voice tinged with sorrow. "But the truth is, we're both connected by this mess. You can't outrun it, not anymore."

Alexander's mind raced. Connected? What was she talking about? What could she possibly have to do with the people after him?

"Emma, what is this?" he demanded, his voice cracking. "What is going on? What does he mean?"

The stranger raised a hand, silencing them both. "Enough questions," he said, his tone low and dangerous. "You'll find out everything you need to know soon enough."

Alexander felt a shift in the air, a moment of tension that was almost unbearable. The men surrounding them, who had remained still up until now, began to move. They weren't rushing in, but their steps were deliberate, calculated, closing in on him and Emma with an eerie precision.

"I'm done playing games," the stranger continued, his gaze now fixed on Alexander. "It's time for you to face the people you've wronged. Time for you to face the consequences of your actions."

A Reckoning

Before Alexander could react, the stranger reached into his jacket, pulling out a small device. It was sleek, black, and he held it with a casual confidence. Alexander's breath caught in his throat.

"This is a simple choice, Moore," the stranger said, pressing a button on the device. "You can walk away, if you're willing to live with the consequences. Or you can come with us and face them head-on. Either way, this is your reckoning."

The device beeped, and suddenly, Alexander felt the air shift, as if the entire world had shifted. The men around them closed in, their movements swift and coordinated. Alexander's pulse raced, his thoughts swirling in a haze of panic.

"Where are you taking us?" he demanded, his voice shaky, trying to hold onto some semblance of control.

The stranger didn't answer immediately. Instead, he gave a slight nod, and the men behind him stepped forward, their eyes locked on Alexander and Emma, as though they were merely following orders. But there was something different now—a palpable weight in the air, a sense of finality. This wasn't just a confrontation anymore. This was something darker, something more dangerous.

"I don't know what's happening," Alexander said, his voice desperate now. "I don't know what I've done to deserve this."

The stranger's lips curled into a cold smile. "You've made your choices, Moore. You've spent years building an empire, but at what cost? You've left a trail of broken promises, destroyed lives. And now, it's time to collect."

The words hit Alexander like a physical blow. He had always known that his rise to power hadn't come without consequence. He had made deals, forged alliances with people who were ruthless, who would stop at nothing to get what they wanted. But he had never expected it to come to this—this reckoning, this moment when his past would catch up with him in the most violent way possible.

But there was more. He could feel it. The presence of the stranger, the coldness in his eyes, the certainty with which he spoke—it wasn't just about Alexander anymore. It was about something much bigger, something much more dangerous.

"We've been following you for a long time, Moore," the stranger continued, his voice laced with contempt. "You think you can hide? You think you can escape from everything you've done? You're nothing more than a pawn in a much bigger game."

A chill ran down Alexander's spine as the realization hit him—this wasn't just about the men he had crossed, the people he had hurt. This was something deeper. Something far more dangerous.

"Why are you doing this?" Emma's voice trembled, but there was a fire in her eyes. "What do you want from us?"

The stranger's expression remained unchanged. He took a step closer to Emma, his eyes never leaving hers. "You don't understand yet, do you?" he said softly, almost mockingly. "It's not about what we want from you. It's about what you've taken from us."

Emma's face paled, and Alexander could see the flicker of realization in her eyes. She understood something that he didn't, something that was unraveling faster than he could process.

"What is it?" he asked, his voice barely a whisper. "What have I taken from you?"

The stranger didn't respond immediately. Instead, he turned, his eyes scanning the men who stood around them. There was a quiet command in his gaze, and the men began to move, their intentions clear.

Alexander's heart raced as he felt the world closing in around him. The reckoning had arrived, and he had no idea how to stop it. Everything he had worked for, everything he had built—it was all slipping through his fingers, unraveling before his eyes. And now, with the stranger's words echoing in his mind, he realized that the cost of his past might be far greater than he could ever have imagined.

Eleven

The Truth Comes Out

The air was thick with tension, each breath that Alexander took feeling heavier than the last. The man in the shadows—the stranger—had spoken, and his words had cut deep, the weight of their meaning settling into Alexander's chest like a stone. His past, his sins, his decisions—everything was coming back to haunt him, and there was no escape.

The men surrounding them hadn't moved, but the stillness between them felt like the calm before a storm, every second drawing them closer to something inevitable. Emma stood beside him, her presence a small comfort in the chaos that swirled around them, but even she seemed on edge, her eyes flickering from one person to the next.

The stranger's voice had echoed through the alleyway, the

The Truth Comes Out

chilling promise of consequences lingering in the air. "You think you can hide forever, Moore? You think you can erase the people you've wronged with a few actions? You can't."

His words had reverberated in Alexander's mind, and now the question burned more fiercely than ever: What have I done?

"Tell me what you want," Alexander said, his voice hoarse with the weight of everything he was trying to understand. He could feel the desperate need for clarity building inside him, a storm that threatened to consume him. "What is it you want from me?"

The stranger took a step forward, the soft click of his boots against the pavement making the air feel even heavier. The streetlights above flickered, casting long shadows that stretched across the alleyway like dark tendrils. The silence seemed to stretch on forever, amplifying every heartbeat, every breath.

"You've been running from your past for a long time, Alexander," the stranger said, his voice cold and deliberate. "But the thing about running is that eventually, you have to turn around and face what's chasing you."

Emma took a hesitant step back, her gaze darting between Alexander and the stranger. The fear in her eyes was palpable, but there was something else there too—a flicker of understanding. She knew something. Something that Alexander had no idea about.

"What does that mean?" Alexander demanded, frustration

lacing his words. "Who are you?"

The stranger's lips curled into a thin, cold smile, his eyes narrowing as if savoring the tension. "You don't remember me, do you?" His voice was almost pitying now, as if Alexander's ignorance was both a weakness and a consequence in itself. "It's been a long time. But I remember you."

Alexander's pulse quickened. He tried to search his memory, to grasp at the name or face that the stranger was hinting at. But nothing came. His mind was a blank slate, the memories fragmented and fading into nothing.

The stranger tilted his head, as if watching Alexander's struggle with amusement. "You were a different man back then, Alexander. A man who thought he could do anything, get away with anything. But what you don't realize is that no one ever escapes their choices. Not really."

"Who the hell are you?" Alexander repeated, his voice sharp, as though the words would somehow force the stranger to give him an answer.

"I'm someone you should have feared a long time ago," the stranger said, his tone flat, devoid of any emotion. "I'm someone who watched you destroy lives and think you were untouchable. But now… now, you'll have to reckon with what you've done."

The truth was still out of reach, and it gnawed at Alexander's insides, unraveling whatever small amount of calm he had left. He could feel his heartbeat in his throat, the pulse of

The Truth Comes Out

panic growing stronger by the second. "You want me to admit something, don't you? What is it? What did I do?"

The stranger's gaze didn't falter. He didn't flinch. "You'll find out soon enough, Moore."

There was no hint of a lie in the stranger's voice. No hesitation. Every word was wrapped in finality, as though the game had already been decided, and Alexander had already lost.

Emma stepped forward then, her hand trembling as she reached for Alexander's arm. "I... I didn't want you to find out this way," she said softly, her voice barely above a whisper. "But it's time, Alexander. You need to know the truth."

Alexander turned to her, his eyes wide with disbelief. "What truth? What the hell is going on? What do you know?"

Emma's lips parted, and for a moment, she seemed unsure, as though the weight of her words was too much to bear. But then she spoke, her voice trembling but firm.

"I'm not just some waitress, Alexander. I'm not who you think I am."

The words hit him like a wave, crashing into him with a force that left him reeling. Emma had been his anchor in this chaotic world—his one connection to something real. He had trusted her. He had confided in her. And now, she was telling him that everything had been a lie.

"What are you talking about?" he demanded, his voice growing louder, his frustration boiling over. "What do you mean, you're not who I think you are?"

Emma hesitated, her gaze flickering to the stranger before returning to him. "I never wanted you to know this. I never wanted you to get involved in my mess. But I can't keep hiding it. I was part of your world once, Alexander. I worked for you. I—" She swallowed hard, her face pale. "I was involved in your company. But not in the way you think."

Alexander's mind was spinning, his thoughts frantically trying to make sense of what she was saying. *Involved in my company? That was impossible. He had never seen her before in his life.*

But Emma wasn't finished. She stepped back, her eyes filled with shame and something darker. "I was one of your employees, Alexander. I worked under you—directly under you. I was part of the team you used to push the company to new heights. But it wasn't just business. I was part of the dirty work too. I did things for you that I wish I could take back. I…" She trailed off, her voice cracking.

Alexander took a step back, his mind racing as the pieces began to click together in a way he wasn't ready for. "No. No, that's not possible. I would remember you."

"You would," Emma said, her voice breaking. "But you never saw me. You never noticed the people doing the work behind the scenes, the ones who got their hands dirty for you. You were too busy building your empire, too busy chasing power, to see the cost of it all."

A silence fell over them, a thick, suffocating silence that hung in the air like a heavy fog. Alexander felt as though the world was spinning around him, his head swimming with confusion and disbelief. The woman he had trusted, the woman he had come to rely on, had been part of the very world he had been running from.

The stranger stepped forward, his gaze unwavering. "Now you understand, don't you?" he said softly, almost pityingly. "You've been running from your past, from everything you've built, but the truth is, it's been waiting for you all along. You can't outrun the consequences of your actions. Not anymore."

Emma's face twisted with regret. "I didn't want this, Alexander. I didn't want you to be part of my past. But the truth is, we're both tangled in it. You can't pretend it doesn't exist. I didn't want to drag you into this, but I couldn't keep lying to you."

Alexander felt the ground shift beneath him. The trust he had built with Emma, the bond they had shared, seemed to shatter in an instant. Everything he had believed about their relationship felt like a lie, and he didn't know where to go from here.

For a moment, he couldn't speak. His mouth was dry, and the words he needed to say caught in his throat. How had he not seen it? How had he not recognized the connection between the woman who had appeared out of nowhere and the world he had been running from?

The stranger's voice cut through the silence. "This is just the beginning, Moore. There's more you need to know. More you have to answer for."

Alexander's legs felt like they were about to give out. The truth was unraveling before him in ways he had never imagined, and it was too much to process. Too much to face.

And yet, the stranger's words lingered, heavy and undeniable: You can't outrun the consequences of your actions.

As the weight of those words settled in, Alexander knew one thing for certain: his reckoning had arrived. And there was no hiding from the truth any longer.

Twelve

The Fallout

The alley was silent now, the only sounds coming from the distant hum of the city beyond, as though the world was waiting for something—waiting for the inevitable. The air was thick with tension, each breath Alexander took feeling more labored than the last. His heart pounded in his chest, his mind still reeling from the truth that had come crashing down on him.

Emma stood a few feet away, her face pale, her eyes wide with regret. She was still trembling, but there was no anger in her—only the quiet weight of guilt, of secrets long kept. Alexander wanted to say something to her, wanted to scream at her for hiding the truth, for lying to him. But the words wouldn't come. They were trapped in his throat, suffocated by the crushing weight of everything he had just learned.

And then, there was the stranger. The man who had been the catalyst for all of this—the one who had exposed the lies and forced Alexander to confront his past. He was still standing there, waiting, observing with cold eyes that seemed to pierce through everything, as if he could see straight to the core of Alexander's soul.

The silence stretched on, unbearable, suffocating, until the stranger finally spoke. His voice was low, almost casual, but there was no mistaking the cold authority in his words.

"You still don't get it, do you?" he said, taking a slow step forward, his gaze fixed on Alexander. "You think you've been running from your past, but the truth is—you've been running from yourself. And now, it's all come crashing down."

Alexander opened his mouth, but no words came. His chest felt tight, his lungs constricted with the weight of what had been said, what had been revealed. He had tried so hard to escape the man he had once been, but now, the truth was clear: there was no running from this. His past, his choices, his sins—they had all come back to haunt him, and there was no place left to hide.

Emma's voice broke the silence, shaky but resolute. "Please," she whispered, her eyes darting between Alexander and the stranger. "We didn't want any of this. We didn't plan it this way. You don't understand—"

The stranger raised a hand, cutting her off, his gaze never leaving Alexander. "Enough," he said, his voice colder now,

The Fallout

sharper. "This isn't about your excuses, Emma. This is about him. About what he's done. About what we know."

Alexander looked at the stranger, his mind racing, trying to piece together the fragmented puzzle of his past. The man's words were like daggers, each one cutting deeper into the very fabric of his identity. Who was this man? And why had he come for him? What did he want?

"You've crossed a lot of lines, Moore," the stranger continued, his tone laced with contempt. "You've made deals with people you shouldn't have. You've built an empire on the backs of others, with no regard for the lives you've destroyed along the way."

Alexander felt the words hit him like a physical blow. His breath caught in his throat as memories began to surface—deals made in the dark, alliances forged in secrecy, people pushed aside for the sake of power. He had known, deep down, that the choices he had made had consequences, but hearing them spoken aloud made it real. It made it impossible to deny.

"Is that what you want from me?" Alexander asked, his voice raw with emotion. "For me to admit what I've done? To confess all my sins? Is that what you want?"

The stranger's lips curled into a thin smile, one that sent a chill down Alexander's spine. "No, Moore. I don't need your confession. I don't need your guilt. What I need is for you to understand that there are people in this world who don't forget, who don't forgive. And you've made the mistake of thinking you could just walk away."

Alexander took a step back, his mind reeling, trying to grasp the enormity of what the stranger was saying. "Who are you?" he asked, his voice barely above a whisper. "What do you want from me?"

The stranger's eyes flickered to Emma for a moment, a brief flash of something passing between them. But then, his gaze returned to Alexander, and there was no mistaking the cold resolve in his eyes.

"You'll find out soon enough," he said, his voice low and dangerous. "But first, you need to understand something. You're not just dealing with me. You're dealing with the people you've crossed—the ones you've wronged. And they don't take kindly to being ignored."

Alexander's heart skipped a beat as the reality of the situation hit him. This wasn't just some vendetta. This wasn't just a matter of bad decisions and misplaced trust. This was something much larger, something that reached deeper into the web of power and corruption that had defined his life.

He looked at Emma again, his mind a whirlwind of conflicting thoughts. She had known. She had been a part of this world—this dark, dangerous world—and yet she had kept it hidden from him. She had kept her secrets, just as he had kept his. And now, it seemed that both of their pasts were intertwined in ways they couldn't escape.

The Fallout

Emma's face softened, a flicker of guilt crossing her features. "I didn't want you to get involved, Alexander," she said softly, her voice breaking. "I didn't want you to know this side of things. But you've been caught up in it now. We both have."

Alexander took a deep breath, trying to steady himself, trying to find some semblance of control in the chaos that was unfolding around him. He had never been good at facing his mistakes, at acknowledging the harm he had caused. He had spent his whole life running from it, pretending it didn't matter, convincing himself that he could be someone else, that he could escape.

But now, as the stranger's words sank in, he realized just how foolish he had been. There was no escaping his past. No erasing what he had done. And the consequences were here, in the form of the men standing before him, in the form of the stranger who had brought everything crashing down.

"Why now?" Alexander asked, his voice thick with disbelief. "Why bring this all up now? Why not let me keep running? Why not let me—"

"Because you're not running anymore," the stranger interrupted, his voice cutting through the air like a knife. "And the people you've wronged—people who have been waiting for you to face them—they don't wait forever."

The words hung in the air like a threat, a promise of things to come. Alexander could feel the weight of them pressing down on him, the realization that everything he had been running from was coming for him with a vengeance. He could no longer hide behind the walls he had built, the lies he had told himself. The truth was out now, and it was unraveling everything he had once known.

"Why did you do it?" Alexander's voice was low, his gaze fixed on Emma. "Why didn't you tell me?"

Emma hesitated, her eyes searching his face. She took a step forward, her hands trembling as she reached for him, but she stopped just short, her gaze faltering. "I didn't want to hurt you," she said, her voice barely above a whisper. "I didn't want you to see me the way they see me. But I… I couldn't keep lying to you. I thought if I kept it from you, I could protect you. But now, I see how much damage has been done."

Alexander closed his eyes, his heart aching with the weight of her words. Damage. That's what they were talking about, wasn't it? The consequences of their actions, the things they had done to each other and to the people who had been caught in the crossfire. The damage was already done, and now, there was no way to undo it.

The stranger's voice cut through the silence once more. "This is your reality now, Moore. You don't get to walk away. You don't get to pretend like none of this matters."

Alexander opened his eyes, his breath shaky as he faced the stranger. "What do you want from me? What are you going to do?"

The stranger's lips curled into a cold, predatory smile. "You'll find out soon enough."

And with those words, Alexander knew—this was just the beginning. The fallout had started, and there was no turning back.

Thirteen

A Chance at Redemption

The weight of the moment hung in the air like a suffocating fog. Alexander stood frozen, the words of the stranger ringing in his ears, each one carving deeper into his soul. The people he had wronged, the power he had used to manipulate and control—it was all coming back to him, crashing down in a wave of realization that threatened to drown him.

Behind him, Emma shifted nervously, her breathing shallow. He could feel her eyes on him, the unease in her gaze, but there was something else there too—something like a flicker of hope. She hadn't given up on him yet. She was still here, standing by his side, despite everything that had come to light. Despite the lies, despite the tangled web they were now both caught in.

The stranger, the man who had been the catalyst for all of

this, stood before them, his posture relaxed but his eyes cold, unyielding. He was watching Alexander, waiting for something, as if testing him. Alexander's heart pounded in his chest, his mind racing. He had been living in fear for so long—fear of facing his past, fear of confronting the man he had become. But now, as the weight of the situation pressed down on him, a flicker of something else emerged from deep within: a chance to do something different, to take responsibility for what he had done.

"I can't undo everything," Alexander said, his voice hoarse, barely above a whisper. He didn't know what had pushed him to speak, but the words felt like the first step toward something he hadn't allowed himself to hope for. "But I can't keep running from it."

The stranger didn't react at first. His eyes were locked onto Alexander, calculating, assessing. It was as though he were waiting for something—waiting for Alexander to prove that he was more than just the man who had spent years hiding behind his wealth and power.

"I've spent my life trying to escape this," Alexander continued, his voice gaining strength with each word. "Trying to bury what I've done, what I've become. But the truth is, I can't run anymore. Not from you, not from myself."

Emma stepped closer to him, her presence steadying him, grounding him in the midst of the storm that was threatening to tear everything apart. Her hand brushed against his arm, a simple gesture, but it was enough to remind him that he wasn't alone in this.

"You're right," he said, his gaze never leaving the stranger. "I've made mistakes. I've hurt people. And I've turned my back on everything that mattered. But I can't undo the past, can't take back the things I've done. But I can make a choice now. I can choose to face it. To own up to it."

The stranger's lips curled into a small, almost imperceptible smile, but there was no warmth in it. It was a smile that seemed to say I'm not convinced, and yet, there was a glimmer of something else in his eyes—something that hinted at the possibility of redemption.

"You think this is redemption?" the stranger asked, his voice low and mocking. "You think you can simply decide to become a better person after everything you've done?"

Alexander felt the sting of the words, but they only fueled his resolve. He wasn't looking for forgiveness—not yet. He wasn't even sure he deserved it. But the one thing he did know was that he couldn't keep pretending. He couldn't keep living in denial.

"No," he said firmly. "I don't expect redemption. But I can't live with the guilt anymore. I can't keep running from the truth. I've spent so many years thinking I could outrun it, that I could build something great and forget what it cost me. But now, I see that everything I've built is built on lies. On broken people. On pain."

A Chance at Redemption

The stranger raised an eyebrow, clearly intrigued, though his expression remained unchanged. "So you've finally realized it," he said softly. "You've finally realized that the empire you built is built on blood. On the backs of people you've hurt. And now you want to make it right?"

Alexander nodded, his heart heavy but his resolve stronger than ever. "I don't know how to make it right. I don't know how to fix the damage I've caused. But I know this—I'm done hiding. I can't change the past, but I can change who I am moving forward. And that starts with facing the people I've wronged. It starts with taking responsibility."

The stranger's eyes flickered briefly to Emma, as though considering something. "And what about her?" he asked, his voice low. "What about the woman who's been dragged into this mess?"

Alexander glanced at Emma, who was watching him with a mix of uncertainty and hope. She had been a part of this world, just as he had, and now they were both tangled in the consequences of their actions. But she had been by his side through it all, even when the truth was ugly, even when he hadn't been the man she deserved.

"I'm not asking for forgiveness from anyone," Alexander said, his voice steady as he turned back to the stranger. "But I need to do this. For myself. For her. I need to show her that I'm capable of being the man she thought I could be."

Emma's hand brushed against his again, this time with more

certainty. "We can't change the past, Alexander," she said softly. "But we can choose to move forward. Together. And we can choose to make things right. One step at a time."

For the first time, Alexander saw the warmth in her eyes, the quiet belief that they could face whatever came next. It wasn't forgiveness. It wasn't redemption. It was something else—something deeper. It was a chance. A chance to rebuild. A chance to take responsibility.

The stranger watched them for a long moment, his eyes hard and calculating. "You think you can change the outcome of this?" he asked, his voice carrying a hint of skepticism.

Alexander met his gaze, the weight of his past pressing down on him, but his resolve unshaken. "I don't know if I can change everything. But I have to try. I can't keep running. And I won't let anyone else suffer for my mistakes anymore."

The stranger remained silent, his face unreadable. But there was something in his eyes—a flicker of approval, perhaps, or maybe just recognition of the choice that Alexander had made. After a long, tense pause, he spoke again, his tone softer, though still carrying the weight of finality.

"You think you can make this right? You think you can change who you are, after everything?" he asked, his voice carrying an edge of skepticism. "I'll give you a chance. But understand this—you'll never outrun the consequences. You'll never erase what you've done. Not fully."

A Chance at Redemption

"I'm not trying to erase it," Alexander said, his voice firm, unyielding. "I'm trying to own it. And that's the first step."

The stranger watched him for a long moment, his gaze unreadable, before he nodded once, almost imperceptibly. He looked to Emma then, as if silently weighing the same questions. Finally, he turned his back to them, his hand still resting on the device he had used to call in the men earlier.

"This isn't over," the stranger said, his voice colder now, like the final, unyielding barrier between them. "But I'll give you your chance. Don't waste it."

And with that, he walked away, the sound of his footsteps echoing down the alley, fading into the distance. The air was still, the weight of the moment lingering between them.

Alexander stood in silence, his heart pounding in his chest. The man who had been his judge, jury, and executioner had given him a chance—a chance to make things right. But how could he? How could he fix everything that he had broken, everything that he had done?

He didn't know. But for the first time, he didn't feel completely powerless.

He turned to Emma, his eyes meeting hers, and for the first time in what felt like forever, he allowed himself to believe that maybe, just maybe, he could be the man she had always seen in him.

"We'll do this together," Emma said softly, her voice steady, unwavering. "One step at a time. We can't change everything. But we can choose to make the next part of the journey count."

Alexander nodded slowly, his heart lighter than it had been in a long time. The road ahead was uncertain, filled with consequences and challenges, but for the first time in his life, he was willing to face it. He wasn't running anymore.

The chance at redemption had come. And now, it was up to him to take it.

Fourteen

A Final Test

The city felt different now. Alexander stood at the edge of the rooftop, his eyes scanning the skyline. The glow of the streetlights below painted the streets in muted shades of gold, while the distant hum of the city seemed more like an echo than a living pulse. It wasn't just the city that felt different. It was him. Everything that had come before—the lies, the deals, the manipulation—it all seemed like it belonged to someone else now. But the weight of those mistakes, the people he had wronged, still clung to him like a second skin, reminding him that the past could never truly be outrun.

The stranger's words still echoed in his mind. You'll never outrun the consequences. It was a stark truth, one that Alexander couldn't deny. No matter how hard he tried to change, no matter how many steps he took toward redemption, there would always be something waiting for him. Something dark, something unforgiven.

And then there was Emma. She had stood by him, through it all. She had been his anchor in this storm, the one person who had believed in him even when he couldn't believe in himself. He owed her everything, but he knew that redemption wasn't just about making things right for himself. It was about making things right for her, too. She had been caught in the web of his lies, pulled into a world she never asked for. And now, together, they had to face the consequences of their actions.

The sound of footsteps behind him broke the silence, and he turned to see Emma walking toward him. Her face was a study in quiet determination, but there was a flicker of something else in her eyes—a doubt, perhaps, or fear. She had always been the one to steady him, to offer him a sense of clarity in the chaos. But now, she was searching for answers just as much as he was.

"You're still thinking about it, aren't you?" Emma's voice was soft, almost gentle, as she reached him. She stood beside him, her eyes following his gaze to the city below. "The past."

Alexander nodded slowly, his gaze fixed on the horizon. "I can't stop thinking about it. About what I've done, who I've hurt. I keep wondering if I'll ever be able to make it right."

Emma sighed, her hand resting lightly on his arm. "You've already started, Alexander. You've made the first step. You've chosen to face it. And that's more than most people can say."

Alexander turned to her, his face a mixture of frustration and

A Final Test

regret. "But it's not enough, is it? I'm still here, still haunted by the things I did. The people I've betrayed."

"You can't fix everything at once," Emma said, her voice firm but compassionate. "But you're doing the right thing. You're facing it. And that's all anyone can ask for."

Alexander closed his eyes, taking a deep breath. He knew she was right. He had taken the first step toward redemption, but that step had led him to a place he wasn't sure he was ready for. A place where the past collided with the present, where every decision had consequences, and where the test of his character was about to begin.

"What's next?" he asked, his voice barely above a whisper. "What do we do now?"

Emma didn't answer right away. Instead, she glanced at the street below, as if searching for the answer in the darkness. Then, after a long pause, she turned to him, her eyes meeting his with a quiet intensity.

"Now, we face whatever comes next," she said, her voice steady. "Together."

Before Alexander could respond, the distant sound of a car engine roared to life, pulling his attention away from her. He turned just as a sleek black SUV pulled into the alley below, the headlights cutting through the darkness. His heart skipped a beat. He hadn't expected them to come for him so soon—hadn't expected the moment of reckoning to arrive so quickly.

"We don't have much time," Emma said, her voice tight with urgency. "They're here."

Alexander's mind raced, his pulse quickening as the realization hit him: the test had come. The consequences of his past were no longer a distant threat. They were here, now, at his doorstep. And it was time for him to face them.

"Are you ready?" Emma asked, her hand gripping his arm as she turned to face him. Her gaze was steady, but there was a flicker of fear in her eyes—a fear of what was to come. But there was something else there, too. Something stronger. Trust.

"I have no choice," Alexander replied, his voice hoarse. "This is it. We face them, or we let them take us down."

They walked toward the door of the rooftop access, the sound of the SUV's engine growing louder as they made their way inside. Every step felt heavy, like the weight of the world was pressing down on him, but there was no turning back now. He had come this far. And now, the final test was upon him.

They reached the stairwell, and as they descended, Alexander's thoughts raced. The people who had come for him were not just anyone—they were the people he had wronged, the people whose lives he had destroyed for the sake of power and ambition. They were the ghosts of his past, the ones who had been waiting for him to face the consequences of his actions.

But he wasn't the same man he had been. He wasn't the man who had built his empire on the backs of others, who had used

A Final Test

people and discarded them when they were no longer useful. He wasn't the man who had run away from his past, hiding behind his wealth and power. He was something different now. Something better. Or at least, he hoped so.

They reached the ground floor, and as they stepped into the alley, the black SUV came to a stop in front of them. The door opened, and two men stepped out. They were dressed in dark suits, their faces hard and unreadable. They didn't look at Alexander or Emma—didn't even seem to acknowledge their presence. Instead, they focused on the man who had emerged from the car behind them.

The stranger.

He stepped forward, his eyes locked onto Alexander's with a cold, calculating intensity. There was no warmth in his gaze, no empathy. Just the cold, unforgiving stare of a man who had come to collect what was owed.

"You're late," the stranger said, his voice low and controlled. "I wasn't expecting you to make this difficult."

Alexander felt his chest tighten as the man's words hit him like a punch to the gut. "What do you want from me?" he asked, his voice steady despite the fear that was creeping into his bones.

The stranger didn't answer immediately. Instead, he looked at the men behind him, who were now moving closer, their steps deliberate, like predators closing in on their prey. They didn't need to say anything. Their presence was enough. The danger was real.

"This is your moment, Moore," the stranger finally said, his voice quiet but filled with an edge of menace. "This is where you prove that you've changed. That you're not the man you were. But understand this: no one walks away from what you've done. No one gets a free pass."

Emma stepped forward, standing beside Alexander, her posture strong despite the danger that surrounded them. "We've already made our choice," she said, her voice calm but resolute. "We're facing this. Together."

The stranger's eyes flickered between them, his gaze briefly softening before hardening once more. He nodded, as though accepting their decision. "Very well. But understand this, Moore," he said, his voice low and dangerous. "This is your final test. You think you've changed. You think you can make it right. But in the end, your actions will determine your fate. And there's no escaping that."

The air between them seemed to pulse with a growing tension, like the quiet before a storm. Alexander's heart raced, but there was no fear in him now. He wasn't running anymore. He wasn't hiding from his past. He had made his choice. And now, he had to live with the consequences.

The stranger stepped back, and with a sharp motion, the men around him began to retreat. Their presence was still heavy, but for the first time, Alexander felt like he had the upper hand. They could intimidate him, threaten him, but they couldn't

A Final Test

break him. Not anymore.

"Let's go," the stranger said, his voice final, almost dismissive. "You've passed the test. But don't think for a second that this is over. The consequences of your actions never truly go away."

And with that, they disappeared into the night, leaving Alexander and Emma standing in the alley, alone.

The city was still there, vast and unknowable, but for the first time, Alexander felt something different. It wasn't fear. It wasn't the crushing weight of his past. It was the beginning of something new.

A chance at redemption.

And for the first time in his life, he was ready to take it.

Fifteen

New Beginnings

The first rays of dawn filtered through the blinds, casting long, thin shadows across the room. The quiet hum of the city outside was a stark contrast to the turmoil Alexander felt inside. He stood by the window, staring out at the streets below, watching as the world slowly came to life. People hustled to work, cars zipped by, and the pulse of the city continued without him, as though everything he had just been through didn't matter. But it did matter. It mattered more than anything.

He wasn't the same man who had stood in this spot days ago, uncertain and trapped in his own choices. Something had shifted. Something had clicked inside of him, like a lock turning, and for the first time in what felt like forever, he could breathe. Not because everything was okay, not because the past was suddenly erased, but because he had made a choice. He had

New Beginnings

faced the darkest corners of his life and walked through them. And now, the world was waiting for him to start anew.

He turned away from the window and looked at Emma, who was sitting at the small table, her face still soft with sleep but her eyes open, watching him. She had been through it all, too. Her past had been as intertwined with his as his own, and yet she had stood by him, unwavering, even when the truth was too much to bear.

Her eyes softened as they met his, and for a brief moment, the weight of the world seemed to lift from her shoulders. She had been there when it all began to unravel, and she had been there when the choice had been made—to face it all, together. And now, as they stood in the quiet of this room, in the early hours before the world awoke, they were starting over. A new chapter. A new beginning.

"We did it," she said, her voice soft, but the truth in her words cut through the air.

Alexander nodded, but it wasn't a victory that brought him peace. No, it was something more personal, more profound. It was the simple acknowledgment that he had faced the hardest thing he had ever done: himself. He had owned up to his past, to the damage he had caused, and now he was standing in the aftermath, unsure of what came next, but knowing that it had to be different.

"Do you feel it?" he asked, his voice rough from disuse. "The change. The shift?"

Emma's gaze didn't waver. She stood and walked toward him, her steps slow, measured, like she was walking through the weight of the moment with him. "I feel it," she said. "But it's not just the change in you. It's in us. We've both been running from our pasts, but now—now, we face it. We build from it."

Her words hung in the air, and Alexander knew, deep down, that she was right. This wasn't just about redemption. It wasn't just about the actions of the past or the consequences they had faced. It was about what they would do moving forward. They had been given a second chance—no, a real chance to build something meaningful, something real. But the question that remained was this: What would they do with it?

He turned back to the window, the city still bustling, the sun now casting a soft golden light over everything. It was as though the whole world was offering a new beginning, a fresh start, just like they were. The weight of his past still pressed on him, but it was no longer suffocating. He wasn't running. He wasn't hiding. He was standing tall, ready to take whatever came next.

"This city," he said softly, almost to himself, "it doesn't care about what happened before. It moves forward, no matter who we were."

Emma joined him at the window, standing just beside him. She didn't speak immediately, but Alexander could feel the weight of her presence, the strength she had given him when he felt most lost. He looked at her and saw the same determination in her eyes—the same resolve to face the future without the ghosts of the past haunting them.

"No," she said finally. "It doesn't care. But that's the beauty of it. This—us—it's about how we move forward. About how we build something real."

For a long moment, they both stood there, side by side, watching the world go by. Alexander could hear the sound of his heart beating in his chest, steady now, like it had found its rhythm again. The knot in his stomach was still there, but it was smaller, less overpowering. There was peace now. Peace in knowing that the past didn't define them—not anymore. The past had shaped them, yes, but it wasn't where they were headed.

He took a deep breath, his eyes still fixed on the horizon. The world seemed a little less daunting now. It was as if he had woken from a dream, a nightmare, and found himself standing in the light of a new day. And with it, came the awareness that he had a choice.

"I don't know what comes next," he said quietly, his voice barely audible. "But I know I'm ready for it."

Emma's hand reached out, brushing against his, and for the first time in what felt like forever, he didn't flinch. He didn't hesitate. He didn't worry about what might happen or whether he was ready. He simply held her hand, feeling the warmth of it, the support of it, and for once, he didn't need to question it.

"We'll figure it out," she said, her voice steady, unwavering. "One step at a time."

And that was the truth, wasn't it? No one could see the future.

No one knew what lay ahead. But Alexander knew, for the first time, that whatever came next, they would face it together. It didn't matter how difficult or uncertain the road ahead was. They had a chance now, a chance to make things right, to rebuild the pieces of their lives, their relationship, and the world they had once been part of.

His past didn't define him. His choices would. The mistakes, the broken pieces—they were part of who he was, but they weren't who he was going to be. He had learned that. And now, he was ready to live with purpose. He was ready to build a future.

"What do we do now?" he asked, finally turning to face her, the question hanging in the air between them, full of possibility.

Emma smiled, a small but genuine smile, her eyes soft with affection. "Now, we start fresh," she said. "Together."

For a moment, they stood in silence, their hands still entwined, as they looked out at the world before them. There was uncertainty, yes. There was doubt. But there was something else, something more powerful than either of those: hope. Hope for a new beginning.

Alexander knew that redemption wasn't a one-time thing. It wasn't about one grand gesture or one single moment where everything was forgiven. No. Redemption was a journey—a long, difficult journey—and it was something he would have to fight for, step by step. But he was no longer afraid of that fight. He wasn't alone in it. And for the first time, he believed that he could make it. He could rebuild.

New Beginnings

They both could.

"Let's take the first step," he said quietly, his voice firm with the knowledge that they could do this together.

Emma nodded, a soft smile spreading across her face as they turned away from the window, their fingers still intertwined, their hearts beating in time. The world outside was vast and uncertain, but for the first time in a long while, Alexander felt like he was exactly where he was supposed to be.

Together.

And with that, they stepped into the unknown.

www.ingramcontent.com/pod-product-compliance
Lightning Source LLC
LaVergne TN
LVHW020423080526
838202LV00055B/5010